Editor
Eric Migliaccio

Managing Editor
Ina Massler Levin, M.A.

Illustrator
Jen Long

Cover Artist
Brenda DiAntonis

Art Coordinator
Kevin Barnes

Art Director
CJae Froshay

Imaging
Craig Gunnell

Publisher
Mary D. Smith, M.S. Ed.

ACTIVITIES for Oral Language Development

Author

Jodene Lynn Smith, M.A.

Teacher Created Resources, Inc.
6421 Industry Way
Westminster, CA 92683
www.teachercreated.com

ISBN-1-4206-3392-9

©2005 Teacher Created Resources, Inc.

Made in U.S.A.

Table of Contents

Introduction

The language arts include reading, writing, listening, and speaking. Much attention is given to teaching and practicing reading and writing. Listening and speaking have long been considered neglected aspects of the language arts. The establishment of standards has brought attention to the importance of instructing students in the areas of listening and speaking. This book provides the classroom teacher with ideas of how to practice and assess speaking skills in the primary classroom.

The book is broken into the following four main sections:

1. **Oral Language Activities**

   The first section provides strategies and activities that can be used within your classroom schedule. Ideas for generating and extending classroom discussions are included, as well as simple ways to get children talking without them realizing that they are talking. The suggestions in this section are ideal for providing practice in speaking, as well as informally assessing students' speaking skills.

2. **Sharing**

   This section describes a variety of ways Share Time can be conducted in the classroom. In addition to a description of a traditional Share Time, suggestions for ways to alter Share Time are included. Letters to parents, as well as some formal and informal assessment forms, are provided for the classroom teacher to track students.

3. **Nursery Rhymes**

   Nursery rhymes compose the third section of this book. This section is ideal to use as you transition students from informal speaking situations to more formal situations. Suggestions for how to assign having students memorize and recite nursery rhymes are provided, as well as parent letters and miniature posters containing the words to several traditional nursery rhymes.

4. **Formal Speeches**

   The final section in this book, Formal Speeches, provides the framework for 10 formal speeches that can be assigned to primary students. Included in this section are a description of each speech, a letter to the parents describing how to prepare for the speech, and a form for assessing students as they give their speeches. If appropriate to a speech, support forms are provided in order to assist students in preparing for their speeches.

Oral Language Activities

Think of an old-fashioned, traditional classroom interaction between teacher and children. It probably goes something like this: The teacher asks a question. "Boys and girls, how do you think Goldilocks felt when she saw the bears?" Ten children in a class of 20 raise their hands to answer the question. The teacher selects Johnny. Johnny answers by saying, "Scared." The nine children who raised their hands put their hands down, and the teacher goes on to ask another question. In this situation, one child is afforded the opportunity to answer. Think for a moment about what the other 19 children were doing. The possibilities might include:

❖ thinking to themselves, "He took my answer."

❖ still processing the question

❖ not knowing the answer or even how to determine or figure out the answer

❖ having a different answer altogether

❖ thinking to themselves, "I know the answer, but I'm afraid to give the wrong answer."

Getting both the teacher and students out of this model of classroom instruction is easy to do; however, it does take the effort of making conscious decisions to facilitate a new way of conducting discussions. The techniques described in this section are designed to be simple ways of generating and extending classroom discussions. Select one or two to implement immediately to generate instant student discussion.

Provided in this section are a variety of ideas for getting kids to talk. Included are activities, questioning techniques, and suggestions for grouping students. Listed below are some of the standards that are addressed as students participate in these activities.

Standards

- Demonstrates competence in speaking and listening as tools for learning

- Contributes in class and group discussions (e.g., recounts personal experiences, reports on personal knowledge about a topic, initates conversations)

- Asks and responds to questions

- Follows rules of conversation (e.g., takes turns, raises hand to speak, stays on topic, focuses attention on speaker)

- Uses different voice level, phrasing, and intonation for different situations

- Listens and responds to oral directions

Classroom Discussions

Why?

It is such a simple question, and yet it often goes unasked in classroom situations. Students often fall into the trap of providing the easiest answer that contains the least amount of words possible. Teachers can easily follow by accepting these short answers. Take the time to ask the simple question "Why?" as a follow-up to responses given in the classroom. Asking this question—especially in response to one-word answers—requires students to explain how they determined the answer or to explain their thinking even further. Now, this follow-up question may come as a surprise to students, especially the first few times you ask it; however, once students know that "Why" will be the next word out of your mouth, they will begin including the "Why" in their responses. Students will begin to elaborate on their answers by including more details or reasoning—which, in turn, leads to better responses. Soon the teacher will not have to ask the follow-up question at all.

Question of the Day

Involve all students in the classroom in discussing a "question of the day." In advance, determine a question of the day. This question can relate to a unit of study, or it can be a random question that you determine. Ask the question to the entire class. Then, have each student answer it. This can be done in several ways. For example, you can simply go around the room and have each student answer the question. Or, you can ask the question when the students are lined up outside the room (for example, out on the playground). Then, when you get to the classroom, stand by the door. As each student comes in the classroom, he or she must tell you his or her answer to the question. A third way is to ask the question to the whole class. Then, take attendance by calling each student's name. The student can let you know that he or she is present by providing the answer to the question rather than answering "Here." To begin with, you may want to limit your questions to responses that require a "yes" or "no" answer. Then, move to questions that require a one-word answer. Finally, move to more open-ended questions that require a sentence or two to answer.

Sample Yes/No Questions

- ✤ Do you have a brother or sister?
- ✤ Do you like the color green?

Sample One-Word-Answer Questions

- ✤ What is your favorite flavor of ice cream?
- ✤ What kind of animal would you *not* want as a pet?

Sample Open-Ended Questions

- ✤ What is your favorite game to play and why?
- ✤ What place would you most like to visit and why?

Classroom Discussions *(cont.)*

More Than One Answer

One of the easiest changes that can be made is a questioning technique that can be used during any time in which you typically ask students questions. This technique works extremely well in all curriculum areas. Rather than have only one student respond to a question, allow several students to answer the same question. For example, when a question is posed (such as, "How do you think Goldilocks felt when she saw the bears?"), have three to five students answer the question. If both teacher and students are unfamiliar with this type of question/answer process, this may feel uncomfortable at first. However, once students get the hang of it, they will not hesitate at all in leaving their hands in the air even after an answer has been offered.

To begin with, allow students to repeat answers that have already been offered by other students. However once students are familiar with this questioning technique, you may wish to challenge them to have their responses differ from responses that have already been offered. In this way, students are required to think of synonyms for responses, reasons that may differ, or examples of how they came to the determination. By allowing more than one student to respond, students continue to think about the question long after the initial response has been given. Due to the extra time that it takes to elicit the students' responses, you will find several benefits. Students' answers become more thoughtful. Students will begin taking more time thinking of and developing their responses because they know that even after the first response has been given, additional students will have the opportunity to answer. Students are forced to think of different ways to express their ideas. Students will begin to listen to each other and build upon the ideas of their peers to develop new responses that often are extremely insightful.

Call a Friend

There may be times when you call on a student to answer a question and he or she does not know the answer. An excellent strategy to use in this situation is to allow the student to call on a friend to help. Ask the class, "Who can help with an answer?" Allow the student who did not know the answer to select the helper. You may even ask the student to call on several friends so that multiple answers can be provided for the question.

A crucial part in using this strategy is then to ask the question again to the original student. The student now has an answer to provide. Depending on the ability level of the student and the complexity of the question or answer, you may allow the student to simply repeat the friend's answer or ask the student to paraphrase the answer in his or her own words.

6

Classroom Discussions *(cont.)*

Think, Pair, Share

"Think, Pair, Share" is an excellent way for students to discuss ideas with other children in the classroom. This discussion technique also provides a way for students to challenge and build upon each other's thinking. For students who rarely share, it initially places them in a less threatening situation than a whole-class discussion, within which they can talk about their ideas. It also front-loads students with answers and/or ideas prior to a whole-class discussion. By talking with a partner prior to a whole-class discussion, all students have an answer or idea to contribute when the whole-class discussion begins.

Initiate this activity by providing a question or topic about which you want the students to think.

THINK

Students begin by spending a few moments thinking about the question by themselves. (Determine the amount of time you wish the students to spend thinking based on the age of the children and the topic about which they are thinking.)

PAIR

Then, pair students. (See page 9 for ideas on selecting partners.) Each partner pair should sit facing each other. The pair then spend the next few minutes sharing with each other their thoughts and ideas. Be sure to provide enough time for both partners to share their ideas and for some discussion that may come out of the shared ideas. As students become more comfortable with sharing ideas with each other and questioning techniques, they will initiate further discussion and questioning on their own.

SHARE

Finally, the class comes back together as a whole in order to share ideas as part of a class discussion. Be sure to let students know that they may share their own ideas or the ideas of the partner to whom they talked. By allowing students to share their partners' ideas, each child in the class comes to the discussion with something to share. Students who seemingly had nothing to share previously have been invited to the discussion because they have a piece to offer, even if the idea was generated by their partner. Chances are that, even if a student shares his partner's idea, he will not repeat word-for-word the exact same sentences. Students often use the idea as a springboard from which other ideas can be added.

During the "share" portion of the activity, the teacher may act as the facilitator or a student may be selected to be the facilitator. If another activity or writing assignment will follow the discussion, you may want to document the discussion by charting student responses. In this way, students are able to use the ideas discussed as part of the assignment. Additionally, students will have access to the spelling of words they may want to include as part of the assignment.

Asking the Right Questions

Sometimes half of the battle in getting a discussion going is asking the right question. Words associated with Bloom's levels of thinking can be used to generate questions that are sure to get students thinking and talking.

Level of Thinking	Key Words			Sample Questions
Knowledge	who	what	where	When did…?
	when	how	define	Can you label…?
	label	show	name	Who was…?
Comprehension	compare	contrast	explain	How would you compare… and…?
	rephrase	relate	summarize	What is the main idea of…?
	infer	classify	interpret	How would you rephrase…?
Application	identify	organize	utilize	What approach would you use to...?
	plan	apply	develop	What examples can you find to…?
Analysis	analyze	categorize	inspect	Can you list the four…?
	conclude	discover	examine	What is the function of…?
	list	contrast	infer	Why do you think…?
Synthesis	theorize	elaborate	predict	Can you propose an alternative?
	imagine	propose	estimate	How would you improve…?
	combine	construct	improve	Can you predict the outcome?
Evaluation	criticize	support	deduct	What choice would you have made?
	evaluate	interpret	perceive	How could you determine…?
	conclude	prove	recommend	How would you explain…?

Forming Discussion Groups

Provided below are several ideas for forming discussion groups. You may find one to work very well for your style of teaching, or you may change the way you select students based on the activity for which you are selecting students.

Tongue Depressors

Distribute one tongue depressor to each student in the classroom. Have students use a black marker to write their names on the tongue depressors. Then, students can use markers to decorate the tongue depressors. Gather the tongue depressors and place them in a can. When you want to group students for discussions with a partner or small group, randomly select the desired number of depressors from the can. Students whose tongue depressors are drawn will work together as a discussion group. Repeat until you have the desired number of groups.

Number Bowl

An alternative to having names written on tongue depressors is to assign each student a number. Cut up index cards into 2-inch squares and write the student numbers on the index squares, one number on each square. Place the number squares in a bowl. When you want to form a group or ask a question, you can select numbers from a bowl.

Name Tag Groups

Determine the size of groups and how many groups you will need to accommodate all of the students in your classroom. Select both a color and a number for each group. Using the colors and numbers you have determined, mark a color dot on the left corner of each student's name tag and write a number in the right corner of each student's name tag. In this way, each student is assigned to two groups, a number group and a color group. When you need students to form a group for a discussion (or any other activity) you have groups already formed. Either call out "color" or "number," and students will group accordingly. You may either randomly or strategically assign students to groups. (For example, you may wish to make your number groups heterogeneous and your color groups homogeneous.)

Pocket Chart

Using a pocket chart to display groupings of students works well, especially if you will be using the same groupings for a long period of time but would also like the versatility of making adjustments to the groups, if needed. Write each student's name on an index card or a piece of cut-up sentence strip. Form groups, based on any desired criterion. For example, you can group students randomly, heterogeneously, or homogeneously. Display students' names in a pocket chart. Place students who will be in the same groups together. If you need to make adjustments to your groups, simply rearrange the index cards in the pocket chart.

Language Experience

If you want to generate instant discussion, try bringing in an object for students to "experience." Creating a language experience is easy to do; and the benefits are far-reaching for generating discussions, building background knowledge, and building related vocabulary. Additionally, through a language experience students learn that what can be spoken can be written down, what can be written down can be read, and what can be read can be thought about.

Depending on your intent for the lesson, the object can be related to a topic being studied, an unusual object that students may have not seen before, or possibly even an object they have seen before. Begin by either placing the object in a position so that all children can see it or by passing the object around for students to experience. Ideally, students should experience the object with as many senses as possible. Although a language experience may be done with the whole class at one time, it is nice to work with a small group. A smaller group provides more opportunities for each student to provide input.

Ideas for Language Experiences

balloon	dust pan	musical instrument	shells
baskets	eye dropper	nest	small toys
berry basket	flower	newspaper	soap
blouse	glitter	pinecone	stamps
bracelet	globe	potato masher	stuffed animal
button	handkerchief	rocks	tortilla
calendar	iron	rubber gloves	tweezers
candle	mittens	scarf	whisk
checkers	music record	sequins	wig

You may choose to let students know that you have a special object that you want them to see and then remain silent for a period to see what conversation the object generates. Students will probably begin talking about the object right away; however, if they don't, you may need to ask some leading questions to get the discussion going. (See page 8 for words that can be used in generating excellent discussion questions.) As students talk about the object, you will want to chart key words that are being included in what the children say. If students are not familiar with the object or with key vocabulary, you will need to provide those critical words.

Language Experience *(cont.)*

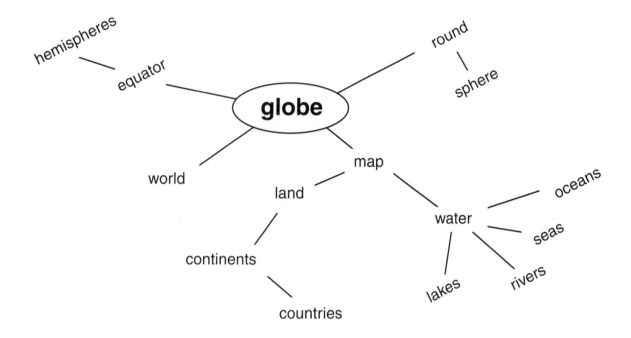

Once the key vocabulary related to the object has been charted, the word chart can be used to help students with a writing piece. For kindergarten students or English Language Learners, this may be a sentence dictated to the teacher. Try writing the dictation on a sentence strip. Students can trace over the letters with a crayon. Then, have students cut the sentence strip up into word cards. Students can practice ordering the sentence and reading it to a partner.

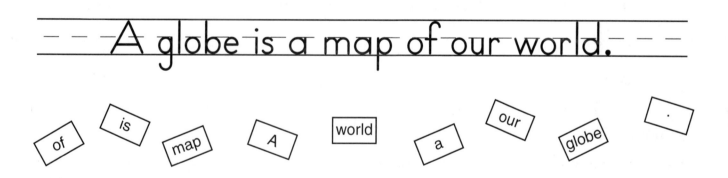

For older students or students able to write for themselves, their writing may be a simple sentence or a short paragraph. Once students have documented something they know or learned about the object, they can draw a picture to go with their writing. The picture may be simply of the object; however, try to have students extend their thinking about the object in a context other than the classroom experience just provided. Students may draw where they might see or use the object in another context. Have students share their writing with the class or with a partner.

Storytelling

I Went to the Store

Seat students on the floor in a circle. Begin by selecting a sound you want to target. For example, you may select the sound /b/. Choose a word beginning with /b/ and say, "I went to the store and I bought a bat." The next student must repeat what you have said, plus add his or her own item beginning with /b/. For example, "I went to the store, and I bought a bat and a ball." Continue around the circle with each child adding to the list. Try to get all the way around the circle. If a student cannot think of a word beginning with the targeted beginning sound, stop, play with that sound and help the student select a new word. If it is a student's turn and he or she cannot remember what a student has said, have the student who stated the word help by providing his or her word again when the time is right.

An alternative to this game is to use the phrase, "I am going on a trip, and I am packing a . . ."

One-Word-at-a-Time

In this activity, the class will collectively create a story, one word at a time. Seat students on the floor in a circle. The teacher will begin the story by stating, "Once upon a time." Then say the first word of the story. The student seated to the right of the teacher then adds the second word. The next student adds the third word. Continue around the circle so that all the students have a chance to add a word to the story. You may even want to go around the circle several times so that the story has a beginning, a middle, and an end. The only rule to this type of storytelling is that the word a student adds has to make sense in the sentence. An example of how this works is below.

Teacher:	Once upon a time, there
Student 1:	was
Student 2:	a
Student 3:	boy
Student 4:	who
Student 5:	had
Student 6:	a
Student 7:	puppy.

Continue around the circle.

Sentence Stories

Sentence stories are similar to one-word-at-a-time stories (see above). Create a story by having each student add a whole sentence rather than just a single word. Once students are familiar with this type of storytelling, challenge them to an alphabet story. In an alphabet story, the first word of the sentence a student adds must begin with the next letter of the alphabet. For example:

Student 1:	<u>A</u> dog ran away from home.
Student 2:	<u>B</u>y the time he got to the corner, he was hungry.
Student 3:	"<u>C</u>ome here, little doggy," called a girl.
Student 4:	"<u>D</u>o you want a bone?"

Continue the story around the circle and through the alphabet.

Storytelling *(cont.)*

Picture a Story

Begin a picture file by cutting out pictures from magazines or newspapers. Provide students with pictures from your file. Ask them to determine a brief story to go with each picture. For example, an advertisement for laundry detergent may picture a boy with dirty clothes. Ask the students to think of a brief story to explain how the boy's clothes got so dirty. This activity can be done with a variety of groupings of students. See below for grouping ideas.

Grouping Ideas

1. Show the same picture to the whole class. Then, students can work with a partner or small group to determine a story. Allow several groups to share their stories.

2. Place students in groups of two or three children. Then, distribute a different picture to each group. Students can work with their groups to determine a story and then share their stories with the whole class.

3. Distribute a picture to each child. Provide time for the child to think of a story to go with the picture. Then, pair the children and have each child share his or her story with the partner. Allow several children to share their story with the whole class.

"What If . . ?" Stories

Encourage students to stretch their imaginations by telling stories to answer "What if...?" questions. An excellent lead in to this assignment is to read the book *Cloudy With a Chance of Meatballs*. This book shows what would happen if it rained food. Create a list of "What if...?" questions. You may choose to generate random questions or relate them to a book that recently has been read or a topic that has been studied. Then, pose a question or questions to students. (See above for grouping ideas.) Provide time for the students to think of their stories. Then, allow them to share their stories. You may also wish for students to draw pictures to go with their stories.

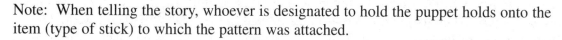

Puppetry

Puppetry is a great way to help children improve their oral-language skills. There are many materials you can use to create puppets. Below you will find five different types of puppets and directions for their creation.

Stick Puppets

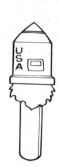

Patterns can be copied onto heavy cardstock or cardboard, cut out, and decorated. The cutouts can then be attached to craft sticks, tongue depressors, paint stirrers, or yardsticks. Don't forget about wooden spoons. Faces can be drawn or glued onto them to create almost instant puppets.

Note: When telling the story, whoever is designated to hold the puppet holds onto the item (type of stick) to which the pattern was attached.

Pop-Up Puppets

The element of surprise is a valuable attention-getting device in the early childhood classroom. Use a cylinder (paper tube), coffee can, or paper cup for the base. Poke a hole in the center of the base and insert a craft stick, sturdy straw, or dowel. Attach an old doll head to the dowel. Use a glue gun to attach the head to the dowel if the dowel cannot be pushed into the head.

Hand Puppets

There are many objects that can be used for hand puppets. If you take some of the stuffing out of a stuffed animal, you will have a wonderful puppet. It is best to remove the stuffing from a slit in the back or the bottom of the animal. Leave the head, arms, and/or legs filled.

Mittens, paper bags, feather dusters, socks, a Slinky®, shirt sleeves, rubber gloves, and kitchen hot pads can all be used to create hand puppets. Use a variety of materials to create the faces of the characters in the story you are telling.

Face Puppets

A face puppet can be created on a paper plate, dust pan, sponge, Ping-Pong paddle, fly swatter, paintbrush, or wooden spoon. Decorate the face to match the characters or animals in the corresponding story.

Finger Puppets

Simple, one-time-only, finger puppets can be made by covering a child's fingertips with masking tape or stickers. Faces can be drawn on the tape or plain stickers. Seasonal stickers, such as pumpkins, can also be used for specific stories or songs.

To make a more permanent puppet, glue felt pieces or pictures to a film canister or cut off the fingers of old gloves and decorate them with a permanent marker or felt details.

Discovery Boxes

Have you ever sat back and watched kids using their imaginations? Imaginations can allow for children to play "house," be rock stars, or even take them to the moon . . . and they have not even left the room. Capitalize on children's use of their imaginations and their willingness to talk to each other while using their imaginations by incorporating discovery boxes into your classroom activities. Discovery boxes are essentially dramatic play centers contained in a box. By placing the items for a theme-related dramatic play center in a box, similar items are stored together and are easily accessible.

Determine one or several types of discovery boxes that you would like to create. (See the list of suggestions below.) Obtain a container in which to store the items. Plastic containers can be purchased from a store, or a simple box will do. Label the boxes so that you can easily locate the boxes and add items to the boxes as needed. Then, begin collecting items related to the themes of your boxes. Once you have a sufficient amount of items for the students to be able to play with the contents, introduce the concept of the discovery boxes to the students.

Show students the contents of the box, one item at a time. Be sure to tell students the name of each item in the box. If students are old enough to read, you may wish to label the items. Demonstrate how you can play with the items of the box. For example, if you assemble an office discovery box (see below for ideas for the contents), you will want to show the students how to use the pens and paper to write letters and address the envelopes. You may wish to type something on the keyboard or make a phone call on the telephone. If you demonstrate for students how to use the items in the box, as well as the correct names of the items, students will immerse themselves into play and language will ensue.

If you have a learning-center rotation, consider making a discovery box one of your centers. In this way, all students will have a chance to visit the center and make use of the items in the Discovery Box. If you have students who are more verbal than others, you may want to take that into consideration when forming groups to play with the contents of the discovery box.

Suggestions for the contents of an office-related discovery box are below.

Office: pads of paper, typewriter, pencil holder, pens and pencils, stamps (music-club and book-club stamps that come in the mail work well), stapler, hole punchers, envelopes, telephones, old keyboards and computers with cords cut off, and pictures of office workers.

Ideas for Additional Discovery-Box Themes

Flower Shop	Gas Station	Fire Station
Beach Party	Repair Shop	Post Office
Veterinary Office	Hardware Store	Dentist Office
Beauty Shop	Grocery Store	Pizza Parlor
Camping	Fast-Food Restaurant	Ice Cream Store
Sporting Goods Store	Doctor/Nurse Office	Bakery
	Police Station	

Share Time

Children love to share! Which teacher has not had to stop a lesson to ask a pair of students to stop talking? Incorporating a Share Time in your schedule capitalizes on children's love for sharing by providing a forum for students to speak. Share time is not a new concept; however, many classroom schedules have squeezed out Share Time due to other curriculum demands.

The importance of Share Time cannot be understated. Although Share Time is not as formal as a speech, it does provide students with practice speaking in front of a group. By bringing an object from home to share, students practice telling about and describing the object. The student who is sharing benefits by learning how to identify important information, organize the information to be shared with others, and become comfortable speaking in front of a group. Rich vocabulary is introduced or reinforced when shared in the context of speaking about an object that has been brought into the classroom. Even if students do not bring in a physical object, sharing about a place they went or about an event in their lives provides excellent practice in vocabulary, as well as in sequencing.

Although Share Time is typically thought of as a kindergarten activity, do not underestimate the importance and interest in sharing, even among older students. Although many kindergarten classrooms do have a Share Time, many do not. For some students, your classroom may be their first opportunity to speak in front of a group. Share Time is an excellent way to ease them into becoming more comfortable.

Standards

Providing students with time to share in the classroom addresses both curriculum standards and student interest. Listed below are oral language standards addressed when students participate in Share Time.

- Demonstrates competence in speaking and listening as tools for learning

- Provides descriptions of people, places, things, and events

- Relates a personal experience using appropriate sequencing

- Uses appropriate body language when speaking

- Uses appropriate eye contact when speaking

- Uses appropriate voice level, phrasing, and intonations when speaking

Share Time *(cont.)*

Share Time Design

The design of your Share Time can take on many different looks. This book provides descriptions, parent letters, and assessments for four different types of Share Time. Select the format of one of these four, or design your own Share Time to best meet your needs.

❖ **Free Choice Sharing** (pages 22–23)

Free choice sharing is exactly as it sounds: students have free choice in determining what they will share. The students determine what to bring as a share item or what topic they will share.

❖ **Topical Sharing** (pages 24–27)

In topical sharing, the teacher assigns a particular topic on which all students must share. For example, the topic for the week may be teddy bears. When students share that week, they must share on the topic of teddy bears.

❖ **Letter-of-the-Week** (pages 28–29)

If you focus on a letter of the week for your letter recognition and phonics instruction, consider tying share time to that letter. By having students bring in objects that begin with the letter of the week for their share item, they are helping reinforce your instruction.

❖ **Impromptu Sharing** (page 30)

Impromptu sharing is a fun way to expand Share Time once students are very familiar with speaking in front of the class. The teacher provides an object or a topic about which a student must speak. The student must then share what he or she knows about the object or topic. The student must do this with no time to prepare or practice.

There are many possibilities for designing your share time. You may decide to select one type of share time and use that format for the entire school year. You may also wish to change the format of your share time throughout the school year. For example, you may start out the year allowing students free choice in what they share. Halfway through the school year, you may want to switch to topical sharing and begin assigning topics on which students must share. Another alternative is to alternate free choice sharing with topical sharing. There are many possibilities. Design your Share Time to best fit both your schedule and your curriculum needs.

Share Time *(cont.)*

Share Time Overview

By establishing and maintaining procedures for Share Time, the time will be spent more efficiently. Establish procedures that best suit your needs. Below are things you may want to consider when determining the look and feel of your Share Time.

❖ When?

If only a few students will be sharing each day, Share Time usually does not take more than 10 or 15 minutes. Share Time can be scheduled at a specific time each day. Students will be anxious to share on their assigned share day. By having a scheduled time, students will be able to anticipate when it is, even if they cannot yet tell time. (For example, they may know that Share Time is after recess.) However, because sharing only takes a few minutes per child, it is sometimes nice to use it as a transition activity. For example, if you are done with a lesson and have a few minutes left before recess, it is nice to have one or two students share during that time. Students are always eager to share, so be sure to allow enough time for each student to share on his or her assigned day.

❖ Where?

You will also want to determine where Share Time will take place. Will there be a special seat for the child sharing, or will he or she simply stand at the front of the room? Will the audience sit on the carpet at the front of the room, or will they sit at their desks?

❖ How?

Once Share Time has been announced, you may want to establish some procedures so that it is as time efficient as possible. For example, if you will be having four students share, you may want them to place their share items on their desks prior to coming to the carpet. By having students place their items on their desks prior to sharing, you do not have a student rifling through his or her backpack while the rest of the class waits for the next speaker. You may also wish to have the speakers for the day line up at the front or side of the room so that the transition time between each speaker is minimal.

❖ What?

What will students say during their Share Time? You will want to teach your students what to say during Share Time. What students will say will often depend on the format of your Share Time. After you have described Share Time to your students, the best way for them to understand what you want them to do is to model for them. Ways to vary what students will say during their Share Time can be found in the sections describing the various types of Share Times (pages 22–30).

Share Time *(cont.)*

Parent Letters

Parent letters are provided for the free, topical, and letter-of-the-week types of sharing. A letter to parents is not provided for the impromptu share due to the format. Sending home a letter to parents about your Share Time helps to keep them informed about what their child is doing at school. A letter helps parents understand what Share Time is and what their child will be required to do when it is his or her share day. A letter also invites parents to participate by helping their child select a share item or topic and then practicing with their child. Parents can also help their child remember when their item will be brought to school. If you will be changing the format of your Share Time throughout the school year, a letter serves to notify parents of the change.

Assessment Forms

Most teachers use Share Time as a format for students to share their thoughts and ideas. A formal assessment has not typically been tied to Share Time. However, district and state standards and standards-based report cards have required many teachers maximize Share Time in order to fulfill these requirements. Many teachers choose to use Share Time as an informal way to assess if a student is meeting oral language standards.

If you do choose to use a formal assessment, a form has been provided on page 20. This form can be copied and filled out as a student shares. The assessment form has been kept very simple so that young children can easily understand it. Because Share Time is usually the first encounter students have with speaking in front of a group, it is essential to keep any assessment that will be shown to the students positive. Focusing on the positive aspects of what a student shares will encourage him or her to be more comfortable speaking in front of an audience again. Write a note at the bottom of the form indicating something that you found interesting. Also, adding a sticker to the top of the assessment form helps keep the assessment positive.

Scheduling Share Time

Scheduling for share time can be done in many different ways; however, in order to ensure students are prepared and to limit the number of students sharing at one time, you may want to assign each student a day of the week on which they may share. By assigning a share day, students do not become bored with a large number of students sharing on the same day. Take the number of students in your classroom and divide them evenly among the days on which you want to allow for share time. You will need to send home a letter notifying families of their child's share day. (See the "Parent Letters" section above.)

You may not want to assign any students to a Monday share day because it is often difficult for them to remember after the weekend. If you do not use Monday as an assigned share day, consider allowing any student to share a sentence or two about what they did over the weekend.

Share Time Assessment Form

Child's Name: _____ Date: _____

Share Topic or Item: _____

	Super Job ☆	Good Job ☺	Needs More Practice ☹
Describes an object or relates a personal experience			
Speaks loudly and clearly			
Stands nicely			
Shows evidence of practicing			

Child's Name: _____ Date: _____

Share Topic or Item: _____

	Super Job ☆	Good Job ☺	Needs More Practice ☹
Describes an object or relates a personal experience			
Speaks loudly and clearly			
Stands nicely			
Shows evidence of practicing			

Share Time *(cont.)*

Assigning Share Time

Crucial to having a successful share time in your classroom is making sure students understand the assignment. The best way to do this is to model, model, model! Before having the first student share—and even prior to sending home a parent letter—spend some time talking with your class about what share time is. Then, model for students what an effective share time looks and sounds like. You may want to consider modeling share time every day for one week before allowing students to share. By modeling, you will establish exactly how you want your share time to be conducted.

It is essential to discuss in detail the types of items you will allow students to bring from home. Establish acceptable and unacceptable items that can be brought to school. Consider school rules related to objects allowed at school. For example, most schools do not allow toy guns. Be specific in providing examples of banned items that will cause the students trouble with school administration.

Be sure students have a clear understanding of how they should transport their share items, where they will store their items until share time, what they will do with them after they are done sharing, and the consequences for not following the procedures. For example, you may want students to keep their items in their backpacks until it is share time and then to directly return the items to their backpacks when they are done. You may also want students to understand that if you see the item at any other time during the day, you will take the item away and that only a parent can retrieve the item. You determine the rules and consequences of how you want to handle these types of situations; however, it is inevitable that these types of situations will come up. By determining how you want to handle these types of situations prior to them happening, and by notifying students of the procedures and consequences, the situation will be handled more easily. Two other things you will want to consider are how to handle large items and animals. You may want to establish a place in the classroom that students can place over-sized items until it is share time. Be sure the other students know the rules and consequences for touching items stored in that place. Also, inevitably, students will want to bring pets to share. Determine in advance your procedures for allowing pets in the classroom.

In addition to modeling what the speaker will be doing during share time, be sure to establish and practice the role of the audience. By making sure students know that the audience plays an important role, you will hopefully deter inappropriate behavior when the children are sharing.

Free Choice Sharing

Free choice sharing is an excellent way to introduce students to Share Time. By providing choices in what students will share, they are often more comfortable when it comes time to share. Students can talk more easily about the things they know best. Enlist the help of parents by sending home the parent letter on page 23.

If students have had little or no experience speaking in front of a group, you may also want to teach students a frame that they can use when they share. By using a frame, the length of their share time and to some extent the quality of their share time is built-in. For example, you may want all students to use the frame below.

Frame:	**Example:**
Good morning, boys and girls.	Good morning, boys and girls.
Today, I am going to share _____ with you.	Today, I am going to share my teddy bear with you.
1. First sentence about the item.	My dad won it for me by playing a game at the fair.
2. Second sentence about the item.	I named her Beary.
3. Third sentence about the item.	I sleep with her at night.
4. Thank you.	Thank you.

Providing a frame does several things. For students who can talk and talk and talk about a topic, it provides a limited number of things that they can share about their item. They will have to carefully select the three most important things they want to say about the item they brought. For students who are usually more brief with what they say, it provides a minimum number of things they must say about their item. As students become more comfortable with the sharing format, you may wish to change the frame or format to better meet the needs of your students.

One way you may want to change the format is to allow the speaker to ask if there are any questions from the class. Establish, beforehand, the number of questions that you will allow a student to answer. Three questions seems to be a good number. Simply explain that there is not enough time for all students to ask a question. If students have additional questions, they can be asked at recess. Wait until students are very familiar with the sharing format before you begin allowing the audience to ask questions of the speaker. This is the first time some students will have spoken in front of an audience. Allow several weeks of practice for students to begin to feel more comfortable before requiring students to spontaneously answer questions. Also, you will probably need to teach students how to ask a question. Inevitably, you will get students who want to comment on what the speaker has shared rather than ask a question. If you only want questions, establish and enforce that rule beginning with the first speaker.

Free Choice Sharing

Parent Letter

Dear Parents,

Share Time is an important time in our classroom schedule. It is an opportunity for the children to share their thoughts and ideas—and, if desired, a special item from home. The children in the classroom get to know each other better by listening to each other share. In addition, by participating in Share Time, students become more comfortable speaking in front of a group.

Your child is scheduled to share weekly on _____. On this day each week, your child will need to come to school prepared to share anything of interest to him or her. Suggestions for share topics are listed below:

❖ a trip   ❖ toys   ❖ books

❖ pictures   ❖ a special talent   ❖ a game

❖ a collection   ❖ a hobby   ❖ a recent event

If your child will be bringing an object to school, please help your child place the item in his or her backpack. The item will remain in the backpack until Share Time. After Share Time, the item will be returned to the backpack. Although the item will be taken out of the backpack only during Share Time, please be sure the item is labeled with your child's name. Also, you may not want to send anything too precious to school.

Please help your child practice what he or she will say during Share Time. Focus on three things your child would like to tell the class. Below is an example of what your child might say if your child brought a teddy bear to school for sharing.

> Good morning, boys and girls.
> Today, I am going to share my teddy bear with you.
>   1. My dad won it for me by playing a game at the fair.
>   2. I named her Beary.
>   3. I sleep with her at night.
> Thank you.

Thank you for your assistance in helping your child prepare for his or her Share Time. Please feel free to contact me if you have further questions.

Sincerely,

_____

Teacher

Topical Sharing

Topical sharing is an excellent transition from Free Choice Sharing to more formal speeches. When you use topical sharing, all of the children in the class share on the same topic each week. For example, one week you may assign students to share about their favorite thing to do with a friend and the following week you may ask them to bring something to share that is the color red. By assigning a topic or a theme, students are required to prepare for a variety of topics over the course of several weeks or for as long as you do topical sharing. Assigning a topic forces students to carefully consider about what they will share. They may have to hunt for an item to bring to school, learn new vocabulary related to the object or topic, or really practice what they will say during their share time.

Consider tying your share item for the week in with a topic you are studying. For example, if you are studying autumn, have students bring in an object that is a sign or symbol of the season. Students could bring in a leaf, an acorn, a piece of clothing they might wear, or an apple. Students and their families are often very creative in thinking of things that make for excellent share items. In addition to practicing oral language skills during their share time, the students are reinforcing concepts and vocabulary that is being taught in the classroom.

Notify students and families of the topic for the following week on Friday so that they have the weekend to think about the topic, practice, and if necessary locate an object to bring to school. Until students are familiar with how this type of sharing will work, you may want to brainstorm ideas with the children once the topic has been assigned. Be sure to chart student ideas. Then, select one of the ideas from the chart and demonstrate how you would share about that item.

Page 25 contains a sample of a letter that can be sent home to parents explaining how topical sharing will be conducted. Once the letter is sent home and parents are familiar with the fact that topics will be assigned, all you need to send home is a reminder of the topic for the week. Pages 26 and 27 contain ideas for a variety of topics that can be used for topical sharing. There are several ways to let parents and students know about the topic for the week. First, if you send home a weekly homework packet, include the topic of the week on your coversheet or on the page with the spelling words listed on it. Second, if you send home a folder with student work in it each Friday, staple the notice to the front of the folder. Third, "reminder bracelets" can be sent home. Write or type the share topic for the week on a piece of paper. If you keep the reminder note brief (one or two sentences), you can create reminder bracelets. Write or type the note several times on a piece of paper. Photocopy the paper as many times as needed so that once the papers are cut apart each student will have a notice. Cut apart the paper in strips so that each sentence is a strip of paper. Staple the strips around the students' wrists to form a bracelet. Inform students that they should not take the bracelet off until their parents have seen the notice. If you will be using the topics on pages 26 and 27, photocopy the page (one for each student). Cut apart the paper on the lines. Send home one topic per week in the form of "reminder bracelets."

Topical Sharing

Parent Letter

Dear Parents,

Share Time is an enjoyable time in our classroom. It continues to be an excellent way for students to develop speaking skills. During Share Time, students are able to share their thoughts and ideas, as well as become more comfortable speaking in front of their peers.

This letter is to inform you that our Share Time will be changing slightly. Beginning next week, students will be assigned a topic on which they must share. Students will still share on their assigned share day; however, students will no longer have free choice of topics on which to share. The topic on which they must speak will be assigned and will vary from week to week. On Fridays, I will inform the class of the topic for the upcoming week. I will keep you informed of the topic via a notice. By knowing the topic ahead of time, you can look for an item related to the topic (if appropriate) and practice with your child what he or she will say.

Attached is a notice announcing the first share topic. Please work with your child to practice what he or she will say during share time. Please do not hesitate to contact me if you have any questions about this change in our Share Time.

Sincerely,

_____
　　　　　　Teacher

Sharing Topics

| **Share Topic** | Favorite thing to do with your friend |

| **Share Topic** | Favorite movie* |

| **Share Topic** | Something pretty |

| **Share Topic** | Something shiny |

| **Share Topic** | Something flat |

| **Share Topic** | Something that is your favorite color |

| **Share Topic** | Something round |

| **Share Topic** | Something you found |

* Students can bring in the VHS or DVD case from their chosen movie.

Sharing Topics *(cont.)*

Share Topic	Something that holds things
Share Topic	A picture you drew
Share Topic	Something you keep in a special place
Share Topic	Something you use when you help your mom and dad
Share Topic	Something that keeps you warm
Share Topic	Something you have shared with a friend
Share Topic	Something smaller than your fist
Share Topic	Something you recieved as a gift for your birthday

Letter of the Week

Many kindergarten and first grade classrooms focus on a "letter of the week" as part of their phonics program. Tie your Share Time in with the letter of the week to help reinforce letter and sound recognition. By having students bring in objects beginning with the letter of the week, they are practicing locating objects beginning with that letter, as well as helping you provide examples of words that begin with the letter on which you are studying.

The "letter of the week" can simply be a topical share (see page 24 for further description on topical sharing). Each week assign the letter of the week as the topic. For example, if you will be studying the letter "Tt" next week, let students know that they must share an object that begins with the letter "Tt."

A fun alternative for the "letter of the week" is to also have the object the student brings be a mystery object. Have students hide the object in a bag or a box and provide clues as to the contents. By doing this, the student sharing gets practice in describing an object, and the students in the audience have an opportunity to interact by guessing the contents of the bag. Both the student sharing and the audience are having the letter of the week reinforced.

Provide modeling for how this type of share will happen in your classroom. The key is to get students to understand appropriate clues that will give the class a hint without actually saying the name of the object. This takes a lot of modeling on the part of the teacher and practice on the part of the students. Below is an example of a frame that can be used to help students with mystery object share.

Frame:	**Example:**
Good morning, boys and girls.	Good morning, boys and girls.
The object in my bag begins with the letter _____.	The object in my bag begins with the letter G.
[*First clue*]	You use it to stick papers together.
[*Second clue*]	It is white and sticky.
[*Third clue*]	It comes in a bottle.
Boys and girls, what is it?	Boys and girls, what is it?
(*Call on three students to guess.*)	(*Call on three students to guess.*)
Yes, it is _____.	Yes, it is glue.
(*Reveal the object in the bag.*)	(*Reveal the object in the bag.*)

If you are teaching in a second grade classroom, tie sharing into a sound of the week. Rather than focus your share time on a letter, focus on a sound appropriate to your grade (such as digraphs or blends).

Letter of the Week

Parent Letter

Dear Parents,

Although we are always learning about all of the letters of the alphabet, each week we focus on one letter. We call it the "Letter of the Week." During your child's share time each week, he or she must bring an object hidden in a bag (or box) that begins with the letter of the week. Your child will provide three clues in order to get the class to guess the contents of the bag. Once your child has provided the three clues for the class, he or she will be allowed to call on up to three students to guess the contents of the bag. If none of the three students guess the contents of the bag, your child will simply show the contents of the bag. Below is a sample of what your child's share time may sound like:

"Good morning, boys and girls. The object in my bag begins with the letter G. You use it when you want to stick papers together. It is white and sticky. It comes in a bottle. Boys and girls, what is it? [Allow time for students to guess.] Yes, it is glue. [Student reveals the contents of the bag.]"

Please work with your child to locate an object that begins with the letter of the week and to think of appropriate clues. Then, practice, practice, practice with your child so that he or she feels comfortable with what he or she will be saying in front of the class.

Thank you for your help.

Sincerely,

_____

Teacher

Impromptu Sharing

Once students become very familiar with Share Time and are comfortable speaking in front of the class, you may want to introduce impromptu sharing. In impromptu sharing, you provide an object or a topic on which students must share. The object or the topic is not revealed until just before the student is required to share about it. Impromptu sharing is challenging because students do not know the topic ahead of time and thus do not have time to prepare. Students are required to spontaneously think of things to share about the topic, as well as to the information for the audience.

Students will be more successful with impromptu sharing if they are familiar with a frame for sharing. See page 22 for an example of a sharing frame. Also, provide topics or objects with which students have had a lot of experiences. Keep in mind the experience levels of the students in your classroom. It may not be appropriate to ask a student to share about a seashell if he or she has not learned about shells or had experience with one.

You may wish to have a box full of a variety of objects. Students can reach in the box and pull out an object about which they must share. Listed below are ideas for objects that can be used for impromptu share.

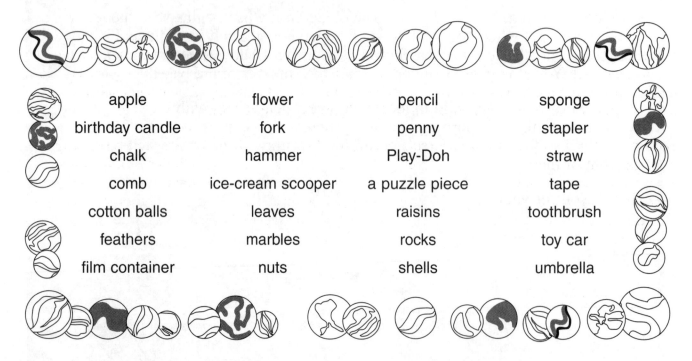

apple	flower	pencil	sponge
birthday candle	fork	penny	stapler
chalk	hammer	Play-Doh	straw
comb	ice-cream scooper	a puzzle piece	tape
cotton balls	leaves	raisins	toothbrush
feathers	marbles	rocks	toy car
film container	nuts	shells	umbrella

Consider using impromptu share at the end of a unit of study as a form of assessment. For example, if you have been studying a unit on Native Americans, you may ask one student to share about housing, another student share about food, and yet another student to share about clothing. Determine the topics for sharing based on the topics you studied. By having students share about topics you have studied, you will get a good picture of the students' understanding of the topic.

Reciting Nursery Rhymes

An excellent transition from sharing to more formal speeches is to require students to memorize and recite nursery rhymes. Nursery rhymes are ideal for this transition for a number of reasons. First, nursery rhymes rhyme. This may sound like stating the obvious; however, the rhyming nature of nursery rhymes assists students in memorizing the poems. Additionally, the location of the rhyming words within the poems—usually at the end of each line or every other line—helps students with correct phrasing of the nursery rhymes. To illustrate this point, try to recite the nursery rhyme "Hickory Dickory Dock" as it is written below. Be sure to pause at the end of each line.

Hickory Dickory Dock

Hickory Dickory/

Dock! The mouse ran/

Up the clock, The clock struck/

One, the mouse ran down. Hickory/

Dickory Dock!

When the poem is written out in this manner, with rhyming words not located at the ends of the lines of the poem, the phrasing of the poem is awkward. The location of the rhyming words at the ends of the lines of the poems assists with the phrasing of the poem. Correct phrasing of the poem lends itself to the sing-song nature of nursery rhymes that makes them easy to remember.

Second, nursery rhymes are short. The short length of most nursery rhymes is ideal to assist young students in memorizing the poem. Finally, many students are already familiar with nursery rhymes. Students who are familiar with the nursery rhymes probably already have them memorized or will need very little practice in order to have the nursery rhyme memorized. For students who are not familiar with nursery rhymes, learning them develops vocabulary and deepens comprehension when the nursery rhymes are referenced in other contexts.

Standards

Listed below are curriculum standards addressed by having students learn and recite nursery rhymes.

- Recognizes the characteristic sounds and rhythms of language
- Uses different voice level, phrasing, and intonation for different situations
- Listens to and recites familiar stories, poems, and rhymes with patterns
- Uses appropriate body language when speaking
- Uses appropriate eye contact when speaking
- Uses appropriate voice level, phrasing, and intonations when speaking

Reciting Nursery Rhymes *(cont.)*

Teaching Nursery Rhymes

Select one nursery rhyme per week that you will teach the children. Write the words to the nursery rhyme on a piece of chart paper or on sentence strips. Display the words so that they can be referred to throughout the week. By charting the nursery rhyme and reading it regularly, students will begin to memorize the words to the poem. Many nursery rhymes have hand movements that correspond with them that also assist students in memorization.

Utilize time spent learning the poem to teach other concepts, as well. Nursery rhymes can be easily charted and used to teach other concepts, such as one-to-one correspondence, rhyming words, sight words, capitalization, punctuation, and any other concepts on which you may be currently focusing. Provided on pages 37–41 are the words to several traditional nursery rhymes. These mini-posters can be sent home with the children so that they will have the words for the nursery rhyme that you are working on each week. Prior to sending home the mini-poster, use it as a teaching tool. Photocopy the appropriate mini-poster. (If desired, enlarge the poster prior to copying and distributing it to the students.) Have students use the mini-poster to practice concepts on which you have been working. For example, if you are working on capital letters, have the students use their orange crayons to circle all of the capital letters in the nursery rhyme.

Parent Letter

The parent letter on page 36 can be used as it is printed or as a model of how to inform parents about the nursery rhyme assignment. Sending a letter to parents keeps them informed about classroom assignments, as well as encourages them to assist their child in learning the nursery rhymes each week.

Scheduling

If you are going to have students recite a nursery rhyme individually, there are a number of ways to schedule listening to each student. An informal way to listen to each student is to call each student to a table at the back of the room and have him or her recite the nursery rhyme to you. This can be done while students are working on another assignment at their desks. You can also circulate around the room and kneel down next to each student's desk and have him or her recite the nursery rhyme to you. Another idea is to take advantage of your guided reading sessions. If you schedule guided reading groups on a regular basis, take the first minute or two of each guided reading session to listen to students recite the nursery rhyme for the week.

A more formal schedule can also be established for reciting nursery rhymes. If students are already assigned a share day, use the same schedule. For example, if a student always shares on Tuesdays, have him or her recite the nursery rhyme for the week first and then share. Reciting the nursery rhyme does not take much time, and the student is already poised to talk to the class for sharing. This maximizes transition time and incorporates the recitation of the nursery rhyme into your existing schedule.

Reciting Nursery Rhymes *(cont.)*

Assessment

This may be the first time students are required to stand in front of the class and recite specific and memorized words. In order to make this a positive experience for students, carefully consider how formally you want to assess students. The manner in which you assess students reciting nursery rhymes may depend on how formally you schedule students to complete the assignment. If you will just be checking to see if students can memorize and recite the nursery rhyme, a simple check-off sheet will be adequate for assessment purposes. A sample of a check-off assessment sheet can be found on page 34. Photocopy the page and fill in both the name of the nursery rhyme and the names of the students in your class who will be reciting it. As students recite the nursery rhymes, assess the areas listed on the check-off sheet. This type of document is mainly used for teacher assessment purposes.

If, however, you are making the assignment more formal by assigning a speaking date and requiring students to stand in front of the class in order to recite the nursery rhymes, you may want to more formally assess their abilities. Provided on page 35 is an individual assessment form that can be used as students recite nursery rhymes. Photocopy one assessment form per student. Complete the assessment form as each child recites the nursery rhyme. The assessment form can be sent home so that both students and parents know how the child performed reciting the nursery rhyme. This assessment form has been designed to be easily understood by young children.

Be sure to discuss with students the standards you will be assessing so that they know what you are looking for. Also, demonstrate for students exactly what you would like them to sound and look like when reciting the nursery rhyme. It is sometimes helpful to purposely model reciting a nursery rhyme in a way that does not meet standards. For example, you may use a very soft voice or look up at the ceiling rather than at the audience while reciting the nursery rhyme. Encourage students to tell you what could be improved in your presentation. By inviting the students to participate in assessing your speaking skills, they become aware of what good speaking looks and sounds like.

Assessment Sheet

Nursery Rhyme: _____

Name	Recites memorized nursery rhyme	Speaks loudly and clearly	Demonstrates good posture	Maintains good eye contact
1.				
2.				
3.				
4.				
5.				
6.				
7.				
8.				
9.				
10.				
11.				
12.				
13.				
14.				
15.				
16.				
17.				
18.				
19.				
20.				

Individual Assessment Form

Name: _____ Date: _____

Nursery Rhyme: _____

	🙂	☹	😖
Knows the nursery rhyme			
Speaks loudly and clearly			
Stands nicely			
Looks at the audience			

Name: _____ Date: _____

Nursery Rhyme: _____

	🙂	☹	😖
Knows the nursery rhyme			
Speaks loudly and clearly			
Stands nicely			
Looks at the audience			

Reciting Nursery Rhymes

Parent Letter

Dear Parents,

We will be learning a variety of nursery rhymes in the classroom throughout the next several weeks. Learning and reciting nursery rhymes is an important component of the primary grades. By learning nursery rhymes, students are exposed to the rhythms and patterns of language. Through our study of nursery rhymes, we will be practicing important early literacy skills such as phrasing, rhyming words, and concepts of print. Additionally, nursery rhymes are often referred to in other types of literature. Familiarity with traditional nursery rhymes will foster understanding when the rhymes or reference to the rhymes are encountered in other contexts.

We will spend time each day learning and practicing the nursery rhyme for the week. After we have learned and practiced a nursery rhyme in class, students will be required to recite the nursery rhyme in front of the class the following week. Most nursery rhymes are short and easy to remember, even if they are new to students. Because we will have practiced the nursery rhymes in the classroom throughout the week, most students will need minimal practice at home. If your child is having trouble remembering a nursery rhyme, help him or her think of hand movements that correspond to the words of the rhyme. The hand movements often help remind students of the words to the poem.

Attached are the words to the first nursery rhyme that we have been practicing at school. Your child is scheduled to recite the nursery rhyme on _____ . Please practice reciting the nursery rhyme with your child at home so that he or she will be ready on the day indicated.

Additional nursery rhymes will be sent home as we study them. Your child will be required to recite the nursery rhymes on the day indicated above. Please continue to help your student practice reciting new nursery rhymes that we will be studying. Please feel free to contact me if you have any questions regarding this assignment.

Sincerely,

_____

Teacher

Mini-Posters

Little Miss Muffet

Little Miss Muffet

Sat on a tuffet,

Eating her kurds and whey;

Along came a spider

Who sat down beside her

And frightened Miss Muffet away.

Mary, Mary, Quite Contrary

Mary, Mary, quite contrary,

How does your garden grow?

With silver bells and cockle shells

And pretty maids all in a row.

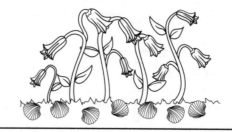

Little Bo Peep

Little Bo Peep has lost her sheep,

And doesn't know where

 To find them;

Leave them alone and

They'll come home,

Wagging their tails behind them.

Hickory, Dickory, Dock

Hickory, Dickory, Dock!

The mouse ran up the clock;

The clock struck one,

The mouse ran down,

Hickory, Dickory Dock!

Mini-Posters *(cont.)*

Old Mother Hubbard

Old Mother Hubbard

Went to the cupboard,

To fetch her poor dog a bone;

But when she got there

The cupboard was bare,

And so the poor dog had none.

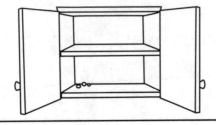

Little Jack Horner

Little Jack Horner

Sat in the corner,

Eating a Christmas pie;

He put in his thumb,

And pulled out a plum,

And said,

"What a good boy am I!"

Peter, Peter, Pumpkin Eater

Peter, Peter, Pumpkin Eater

Had a wife and couldn't keep her;

He put her in a pumpkin shell,

And there he kept her very well.

Jack Be Nimble

Jack be nimble.

Jack be quick.

Jack jump over the candlestick.

38

Mini-Posters *(cont.)*

The Three Little Kittens

The three little kittens,

They lost their mittens,

And they began to cry.

"Oh, mother dear, we sadly fear,

Our mittens we have lost."

"What! Lost your mittens, you

  naughty kittens!

Then you shall have no pie."

The Itsy Bitsy Spider

The itsy bitsy spider

Climbed up the water spout.

Down came the rain

And washed the spider out.

Out came the sun

And dried up all the rain.

And the itsy bitsy spider

Climbed up the spout again.

Humpty Dumpty

Humpty Dumpty sat on a wall.

Humpty Dumpty had a great fall.

All the king's horses

And all the king's men,

Couldn't put Humpty

Together again.

Little Boy Blue

Little Boy Blue, come blow
your horn,

The sheep's in the meadow, the
cow's in the corn;

But where is the boy who looks
after the sheep?

He's under the haystack
fast asleep.

Mini-Posters *(cont.)*

Hey Diddle, Diddle

Hey diddle, diddle

The cat and the fiddle,

The cow jumped over the moon.

The little dog laughed
to see such sport,

And the dish ran away
with the spoon.

Pease Porridge

Pease porridge hot,

Pease porridge cold,

Pease porridge in the pot,
nine days old.

Some like it hot,

Some like it cold,

Some like it in the pot,
nine days old.

Mary Had a Little Lamb

Mary had a little lamb,

Whose fleece was white as snow;

And everywhere that Mary went

The lamb was sure to go.

Jack and Jill

Jack and Jill went up the hill,

To fetch a pail of water.

Jack fell down, and
broke his crown,

And Jill came tumbling after.

Mini-Posters *(cont.)*

Baa, Baa, Black Sheep

Baa, Baa, black sheep,

Have you any wool?

Yes, sir, yes, sir,

Three bags full;

One for my master,

One for my dame,

And one for the little boy

Who lives down the lane.

The Old Woman Who Lived in a Shoe

There was an old woman

Who lived in a shoe.

She had so many children,

She didn't know what to do.

She gave them some broth

Along with some bread,

Then hugged them all soundly

And sent them to bed.

Little Betty Blue

Little Betty Blue

Lost her holiday shoe,

What can little Betty do?

Give her another

To mach the other,

And then she may walk in two.

Star Light, Star Bright

Star light, star bright,

First star I see tonight,

I wish I may, I wish I might,

Have the wish I wish tonight.

Speech Assignments

Assigning formal speeches is another way of helping students develop oral language skills. Provided in this section are 10 formal speech assignments. The speech assignments are designed with specific components that students practice at home and then present on an assigned day. Below is a list of speech assignments included in this section:

❖ **Introduction Speech**

❖ **Favorite Things Speech**

❖ **Mystery Object Speech**

❖ **Demonstration Speech**

❖ **Personal Information Speech**

❖ **Joke Speech**

❖ **Book Talk Speech**

❖ **Patriotic Speech**

❖ **Reciting-a-Poem Speech**

❖ **Favorite Memory Speech**

Most of the speeches can be assigned at any point during the school year. However, it is recommended that the Introduction Speech be assigned first because it lays the groundwork for information that is included as part of the other speeches. Also, it is recommended that the Favorite Memory Speech be assigned at the end of the school year because it requires students to select a favorite memory from the school year.

Standards

The formal speeches included in this section were designed to address both curriculum standards and student interest. Listed below are standards addressed in the speech assignments within this section:

All Formal Speech Assignments:
- Uses appropriate body language when speaking
- Uses appropriate eye contact when speaking
- Uses appropriate voice level, phrasing, and intonations when speaking

Book Talk Speech:
- Identifies setting, main characters, main events, and problems in stories
- Identifies favorite books and stories
- Applies reading skills and strategies to a variety of familiar literary passages and texts

Patriotic Speech and Reciting-a-Poem Speech:
- Listens to and recites familiar stories, poems, and rhymes with patterns
- Recognizes the characteristic sounds and rhythms of language

All Remaining Speeches:
- Provides descriptions of people, places, things, and events

Speech Assignments *(cont.)*

Speech Design

Each speech assignment within this section contains three basic pages essential to the assignment: a speech overview for the teacher, a parent letter that explains the speech assignment to parents, and an assessment sheet. Support pages are also included for some assignments. The support pages provide extra structure for students to assist when practicing the components of the speech.

Speech Overview

The first page of each speech assignment provides an overview for the teacher. Included is an introduction to the assignment, a description of the speech requirements, and tips for helping students be successful on the assignment. If appropriate, additional pages follow this overview page that are designed to help guide students through the assignment. These pages are generally designed to be classroom activities. Once completing the activities in the classroom, students can take the completed activity home to act as a guide when practicing their speech.

Parent Letter

The parent letters provide both parents and students with the speech assignment. A description of the components of the speech is provided on each letter, as well as an example of what a student's speech may sound like. The letters also encourage parents to practice with their child.

There is a place for the teacher to sign his or her name at the bottom of the parent letter. Be sure to place your signature on the letter prior to photocopying and distributing the letter. Each parent letter also indicates that a copy of the assessment used to evaluate students will be sent home with the parent letter. Be sure to photocopy the assessment form on the back or staple a copy of the assessment form to the parent letter.

A calendar is provided at the bottom of each parent letter. See the section on scheduling speeches on the next page for a description on how to use this calendar. Be sure to fill in this section prior to photocopying and distributing the speech assignment.

Assessment Forms

The final page, which is common to each speech assignment, is an oral language assessment. Although the format for each oral language assessment is similar, there are slight variations in each form that address the specific components of each speech. The format has been kept simple so students will understand the assessment form. The form is designed in a check-off format to indicate whether each component of the speech was addressed. There is space at the bottom of each form for comments.

Speech Assignments *(cont.)*

Assigning Speeches

When assigning a formal speech, be sure to provide plenty of time to explain to students the requirements of the speech. If it is appropriate to the students with whom you are working, you may wish to distribute the parent letter to students or write the components of the speech on the board or a piece of chart paper so that students can follow along. If you will be guiding students through the speech assignment (for example, on the Book Talk Speech), explain to students exactly how each mini assignment will work together to result in the assigned speech.

Model, model, model! Demonstrate exactly what students' speeches should sound like. Make up your own speech based on the criteria listed for the speech that is being assigned or read the sample that is provided on the parent letter. Either way, students should be provided with at least one example of how this speech will sound. You may also wish to distribute a copy of the assessment form that you will be using. Have students follow along on the assessment form as you model what the speech will sound like. You may even wish to have them fill out an assessment on you as you provide your example.

If students are new to seeing formal assessment forms such as the ones provided in this book, provide them with several opportunities to assess you as you model excellent versions of the speech and versions of the speech that may need some improvement. By practicing filling out the assessment form, students will better know and understand what you will be looking for when you complete an assessment form on the speech they give.

Scheduling Speeches

Be sure to provide students their speech assignments so they have plenty of time to prepare for and practice the components of the speech. A blank calendar is provided at the bottom of each parent letter. It is recommended that you complete the calendar for the month in which the speech is assigned. Then, assign two to three children a day to give their speeches. Simply write the students' names on the day on which you wish them to present their speeches. (See the sample to the right.) By limiting the number of speeches in a day, audience interest in listening to the speeches will not be compromised. The following month, rotate the students who were assigned to give their speeches early to a space later in the week or month so that the same children do not always have to be first.

April

Monday	Tuesday	Wednesday	Thursday	Friday
		1	2	3
6	7	8	9	10
13 Sophia Frank	14 Neil Ana	15 Nicky Andrew	16 Alex Jane	17 Wendy Jose
20 Max Ella	21 Mark Stan	22 Kyle Kris	23 Eva Todd	24 Joy Lisa
27	28	29	30	

If students in your classroom already have an assigned day on which they share, you may wish to use that time for students to give their speeches. Simply select a week in which you want students to give their speeches. Notify parents that during that week, students will be required to give their speeches to the class rather than sharing.

Introduction Speech

Introduction

An introduction speech is an excellent first formal speech. There is a limited number of requirements for this speech and the required components are personal pieces of information that most students already know. Using this introduction speech as your first speech accomplishes two things. First, students become familiar with the idea of speaking formally in front of the class. This also may be the first time your students have had an experience with a speaking assessment. Students will become familiar with how you are going to assess them, too. Second, the first several components of this introduction speech are used as an introduction to other speeches in this book. Becoming comfortable with these components helps with student success on other speeches.

Assignment

Students begin this speech by presenting basic information about themselves. Students should state their complete names, dates, ages, and birthdates. Finally, students will state a few sentences telling about their family.

Speech Components

- ❖ Student's complete name (first name and last name, middle name if desired)

- ❖ Today's date (the date of the speech)

- ❖ Student's age

- ❖ Student's date of birth (month, day, and year)

- ❖ At least two sentences telling about the student's family

☞ Tips for Student Success

Stating their names, ages, and birth dates will probably be easy for many children in your classroom. Additionally, most children know enough about their families to be successful telling about their families, even if they have not practiced. The most challenging component of this speech is stating the date (the date of the speech).

Each day introduction speeches are scheduled, begin the day by writing the date on a piece of chart paper, a sentence strip, or on the board. This activity can easily be incorporated into calendar activities for the day. Practice reading the date several times, and then display the date in a place where students presenting their speeches can see it, if need be.

Introduction Speech
Parent Letter

Dear Parents,

Presenting a formal speech is an excellent opportunity for students to develop oral language skills and to become comfortable speaking in front of a group. For this speech assignment, students will be required to present the items listed below. An example of what your child's speech may sound like is also below.

1. Child's first and last name (and middle name, if desired)

2. Today's complete date (day, month, date, and year of the speech)

3. Child's age

4. Child's birth date (month, day, and year)

5. At least two sentences describing, explaining, or telling something about the child's family.

Example:

"Good morning, boys and girls. My name is Kyle Anderson. Today is Tuesday, September 20, 2005. I am six years old, and my birthday is September 1, 1999. There are five people in my family. I have a mom and a dad, an older brother named Joshua, and a baby sister named Sarah. Do you have any questions?"

Attached is a sample of the evaluation sheet that will be used in assessing your child's speech. Please help your child practice the items listed above so that he or she is prepared for his or her presentation on the date noted on the calendar below.

Sincerely,

_____

Teacher

Monday	Tuesday	Wednesday	Thursday	Friday

Introduction Speech

Oral Language Assessment

Student's Name: _____

Speech Components

Yes	No	Item
		States first and last name
		States complete date
		States age
		States complete birthdate
		Shares at least two sentences describing, explaining, or telling something about family

Oral Language Presentation Components

Yes	Needs Improvement	No	Item
			Speaks clearly
			Has good voice projection
			Has good eye contact
			Has good posture
			Shows evidence of having practiced the speech at home

Comments: _____

_____

_____

Favorite Things Speech

Introduction

A Favorite Things Speech is another great speech to use when introducing formal speaking to students. For this speech, students are able to select a favorite thing about which to speak. Most children have little difficulty coming up with a favorite thing to share with the class. Students can select any favorite thing that is appropriate to speak about in a classroom setting. You may want to encourage students to bring their favorite things to school, if possible.

Assignment

Students will begin this speech by presenting basic introduction information, including their complete names and the date. Students will then speak about something that is their favorite. The topic of their favorite things speech does not matter. Almost any topic will work (favorite animal, color, game, movie, book, etc.). Students are required to share at least three sentences in order to describe, explain, or tell more about their favorite things.

Speech Components

❖ Student's complete name (first name and last name, middle name if desired)

❖ Today's date (the date of the speech)

❖ A favorite thing (any type of favorite thing can be used for this speech)

❖ At least three sentences describing, explaining, or telling more about the favorite thing. (Use the worksheet on page 50 to guide students through the process of telling more about their favorite thing.)

☞ Tips for Student Success

Guiding students through the student worksheet will provide an excellent outline for their speeches. After helping students complete the "Favorite Things Worksheet," allow them to practice presenting about their favorite thing to a partner. While practicing, allow students to have the worksheet in front of them in order to use it as a guide for what to say.

On another day, have students practice presenting about their favorite thing to a partner again. This time, allow students to have the "Favorite Things Worksheet" in front of them; however, encourage students to place it face down on the desk and use it only if necessary.

Favorite Things Speech *(cont.)*

Teacher's Guide to the Worksheet

Materials

- a piece of chart paper or a white board
- a copy of page 50, one per student

Brainstorming Favorites

Write the word "favorites" in the middle of a piece of chart paper or the white board. Circle the word. Ask students to brainstorm categories of things that could be favorites. See the sample for what your list may look like, as well as categories you may want to be sure your students include. Help students keep the categories broad. For example, if a student suggests the word "dogs," tell the student that a dog is a type of animal. Chart the word "animal" instead of the word "dog."

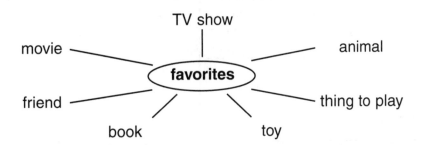

Using the Worksheet

Distribute a copy of page 50, one per student. Have students use the brainstorming web to complete the first part of the worksheet, the section on the category. Students can complete the sentence provided about their favorite thing, or they can write their own.

Assist students in narrowing down their category to a specific example of the category. In the example provided, the category is "animals." The topic is "dogs." Once again, students can either complete the sentence frame provided on the worksheet or they can write their own sentence.

Use the remaining three boxes for students to provide specific examples of why they like their favorite thing. Have students write a sentence on the left side of the page and draw a picture that will assist them in remembering their example on the right side of the page.

Favorite Things Speech
Student Worksheet

Favorite Thing: _____ animals _____

I would like to tell you about my favorite <u>animal</u>.

My favorite <u>animal</u> is a <u>dog</u>.

<u>Dogs are happy to see you when you come home.</u>	
<u>They love to chew on bones.</u>	
<u>My dogs are Boomba and Spike.</u>	

Favorite Things Speech

Student Worksheet

Favorite Thing: _____
(category)

I would like to tell you about my favorite thing.

My favorite _____ is _____.
(category)   (topic)

Sentence about topic: _____ _____ _____ _____ _____	Picture
Sentence about topic: _____ _____ _____ _____ _____	Picture
Sentence about topic: _____ _____ _____ _____ _____	Picture

Favorite Things Speech

Parent Letter

Dear Parents,

Presenting a formal speech is an excellent opportunity for students to develop oral language skills and to become comfortable speaking in front of a group. On this speech assignment, students will be required to present the items listed below. An example of what your child's speech may sound like is also below.

1. Child's first and last name (middle name, if desired)

2. Today's complete date (day, month, date, and year of the speech)

3. A favorite thing

4. At least three sentences describing, explaining, or telling more about the favorite thing

The children have completed a worksheet in school to help them select a favorite thing about which to speak, as well as some details that describe, explain, or tell more about their favorite thing. Use this worksheet as a guide when practicing your child's speech with him or her.

Example:

"Good morning, boys and girls. My name is Hollie McDonall. Today is Wednesday, October 12, 2005. I would like to tell you about my favorite animal. My favorite animal is a dog. Dogs are always happy to see you when you come home. They love to chew on bones. My family has two dogs. One dog is a pug named Boomba, and the other dog is a golden retriever named Spike. Both of my dogs love to play with me. Do you have any questions?"

Attached is a sample of the evaluation sheet that will be used in assessing your child's speech. Please help your child practice the items listed above so that he or she is prepared for his/her presentation on the date noted on the calendar.

Sincerely,

_____

Teacher

Monday	Tuesday	Wednesday	Thursday	Friday

Favorite Things Speech

Oral Language Assessment

Student's Name: _____

Speech Components

Yes	No	Item
		States first and last name
		States complete date
		States the category and topic of the favorite thing
		Shares at least three sentences describing, explaining, or telling more about the topic

Oral Language Presentation Components

Yes	No	Item
		Speaks clearly
		Has good voice projection
		Has good eye contact
		Has good posture
		Shows evidence of having practiced the speech at home

Comments: _____

_____

_____

Mystery Object Speech

Introduction

A Mystery Object Speech will become one of your students' favorite types of oral language presentations. The speakers love the mystery aspect of bringing a hidden object. The audience loves to participate in the presentation by guessing the contents of the bag. An additional benefit of this type of speech is providing students with an opportunity to practice giving appropriate clues that will guide the listener to the correct answer without actually telling them the mystery object.

Assignment

Students begin this speech by presenting basic introduction information, including their complete names and the date. Additionally, students will bring a mystery object hidden in a bag and provide three clues as to the contents of the bag. The class will be asked to guess the contents of the bag based on the clues that are provided. Finally, students will provide a few sentences explaining why they chose the object that they brought to school.

Speech Components

- ❖ Student's complete name (first name and last name, middle name if desired)

- ❖ Today's date (the date of the speech)

- ❖ Three clues about a mystery object

- ❖ At least two sentences describing, explaining, or telling more about the object once it is revealed

☞ Tips for Student Success

Students often struggle with providing appropriate clues that will help the audience correctly identify the mystery object. For example, if the mystery object is a stuffed frog, a clue that would help is, "The object is green." A clue that would not help is, "The object's name is Simon." Help students practice identifying the three most important clues that will lead the audience to identify an object prior to assigning the speech.

Play the game "I spy" with your students. In the game "I Spy," the speaker identifies an object that he or she can see, and then provides students with clues for guessing the object. For example, the speaker could say, "I spy something in our classroom that is blue. It has four legs, people sit on it, and each child has one at his or her desk." Students try to guess that the object is a chair. This is an excellent way to spend those five minutes before recess or while waiting in the lunch line.

Mystery Object Speech

Parent Letter

Dear Parents,

Presenting a formal speech is an excellent opportunity for students to develop oral language skills and to become comfortable speaking in front of a group. For this speech assignment, students will be required to present the items listed below. An example of what your child's speech may sound like is also below.

- Child's first and last name (middle name, if desired)

- Today's complete date (day, month, date, and year of the speech)

- An object hidden in a bag. Your child must give the letter of the alphabet that the object begins with and three clues describing that object so that the class can guess what is in the bag.

- At least two sentences describing, explaining, or telling something about the object in the bag

Example:

"Good morning, boys and girls. My name is Alexis Avila. Today is Monday, November 14, 2005. The object in my bag begins with the letter L. It is green. It grows on a tree. In the fall it turns yellow and red. Boys and girls, what is it?" (Provide time for students to guess the answer: a leaf.) "I found this leaf in my front yard. I decided to pick it up because I liked the shape of it. Do you have any questions?"

Attached is a sample of the evaluation sheet that will be used in assessing your child's speech. Please help your child practice the items listed above so that he or she is prepared for his or her presentation on the date noted on the calendar.

Sincerely,

_____
Teacher

Monday	Tuesday	Wednesday	Thursday	Friday

Mystery Object Speech

Oral Language Assessment

Student's Name: _____

Speech Components

Yes	No	Item
		States first and last name
		States complete date
		Gives three clues to accurately describe a mystery object
		Shares at least two sentences describing, explaining, or telling more about the object

Oral Language Presentation Components

Yes	Needs Improvement	No	Item
			Speaks clearly
			Has good voice projection
			Has good eye contact
			Has good posture
			Shows evidence of having practiced the speech at home

Comments: _____

_____

Personal Information Speech

Introduction

Although having students demonstrate knowledge of their own phone numbers and street addresses is not a standard in many states, teachers often require their students to memorize this information because of how crucial the knowledge of this information is for student safety. By incorporating memorizing this information into a formal speech, students learn their phone numbers and addresses and they practice speaking skills at the same time.

Assignment

Students begin this speech by presenting basic introduction information including their complete name and the date. Students will also recite their complete telephone numbers and street addresses.

Speech Components

❖ Student's complete name (first name and last name, middle name if desired)

❖ Today's date (the date of the speech)

❖ Student's complete phone number, including area code

❖ Student's complete street address, including city, state, and zip code

☞ ## Tips for Student Success

Students will fall into a couple of categories with their prior knowledge of the components of this speech. Some students will already know all of the information required and simply need to practice reciting it in a more formal way. Many students will know part of the information required. For example, many students already know their phone numbers; however, they never learned their area codes. Finally, for some students, learning their personal information will be new to them.

Photocopy the telephone and house patterns provided on page 57. Complete a sheet for each student by writing each child's complete name, phone number, and address in the appropriate places in the patterns. Tape the sheet to the students' desks prior to assigning this speech. This can be done as far in advance of assigning the speech as you think is appropriate for your students. Explain to the children that this is their address and phone number, and they will need to learn this information. By having the pattern taped to their desks, students are reminded daily of the requirement to learn the information, as well as the correct information that they should be memorizing. You may wish to check with parents ahead of time to be sure you have accurate personal information.

Personal Information Speech

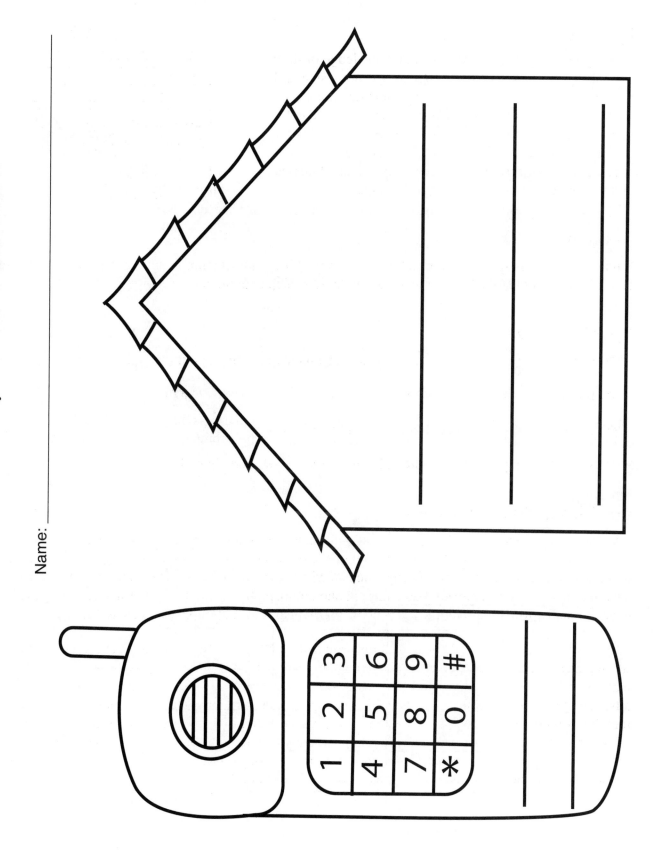

Telephone and House Patterns

Name: _____

Personal Information Speech

Parent Letter

Dear Parents,

Presenting a formal speech is an excellent opportunity for students to develop oral language skills and to become comfortable speaking in front of a group. For this speech assignment, students will be required to present the items listed below. An example of what your child's speech may sound like is also below.

1. Child's first and last name (middle name, if desired)

2. Today's complete date (day, month, date, and year of the speech)

3. Child's complete phone number, including area code

4. Child's complete street address, including city, state, and zip code

Example:

"Good morning, boys and girls. My name is Steffi Montes. Today is Monday, December 12, 2005. My phone number is (555) 555-5555. My street address is 555 Main Street, Los Angeles, California 55555. Thank you."

Attached is a sample of the evaluation sheet that will be used in assessing your child's speech. Please help your child practice the items listed above so that he or she is prepared for his or her presentation on the date noted on the calendar.

Sincerely,

_____

Teacher

Monday	Tuesday	Wednesday	Thursday	Friday

Personal Information Speech

Oral Language Assessment

Student's Name: _____

Speech Components

Yes	No	Item
		States first and last name
		States complete date
		States complete phone number, including area code
		States complete street address, including city, state, and Zip code

Oral Language Presentation Components

Yes	Needs Improvement	No	Item
			Speaks clearly
			Has good voice projection
			Has good eye contact
			Has good posture
			Shows evidence of having practiced the speech at home

Comments: _____

_____

_____

Joke Speech

Introduction

Elementary-school children are at an age where they are beginning to have a better command of words and language. Many jokes for children are funny because the punchline is a play on words. Students this age are just beginning to appreciate and "get" the joke because of their increasing understanding of the English language. After presenting this speech, you will often find that children begin making up their own jokes.

Assignment

Students begin this speech by presenting basic introduction information, including their complete name and the date. Students will also tell a joke to the class.

Speech Components

❖ Student's complete name (first name and last name, middle name if desired)

❖ Today's date (the date of the speech)

❖ A joke appropriate for K-2 children. (You may wish to select 8–10 jokes from which students can select and type them on a piece of paper. Attach the selection of jokes to the parent letter.)

☞ Tips for Student Success ─────────────────────

The most difficult part of presenting this speech is the timing of telling the punchline after the initial part of the joke has been told. The easiest way to help students understand the timing of the punchline is to model, model, model. Check out joke books from the library or locate jokes on the Internet. (Some suggested websites are listed below.) Be sure to screen any jokes prior to telling them to children. Spend the weeks prior to assigning this speech, telling jokes to your class, modeling appropriate timing of the punchline. Telling a joke is an excellent way to spend those two minutes while you are waiting for the recess bell to ring.

Books

Johnstone, Michael. *1,000 Crazy Jokes for Kids*. Ballentine Books, 1988.

Keller, Charles. *The Little Giant Book of Knock, Knocks*. Sterling Publishing, 1997.

Lewman, David. *Joke Book*. Simon Spotlight, 2000.

Web Sites

http://halife.com/family/kids/kackles.html

http://kidhumor.glowport.com/

http://surfsafely.com/directory/Entertainment/Jokes/

Joke Speech

Parent Letter

Dear Parents,

Presenting a formal speech is an excellent opportunity for students to develop oral language skills and to become comfortable speaking in front of a group. For this speech assignment, students will be required to present the items listed below. An example of what your child's speech may sound like is also below.

1. Child's first and last name (middle name, if desired)

2. Today's complete date (day, month, date, and year of the speech)

3. Recite a joke

Please be sure that the joke your child selects is appropriate to tell to K-2 children.

Example:

"Good morning, boys and girls. My name is Andy Del Rosario. Today is Monday, January 24, 2005. I would like to tell you a joke. Why did the chicken cross the playground? [*Pause for a moment.*] To get to the other slide. Thank you."

Attached is a sample of the evaluation sheet that will be used in assessing your child's speech. Please help your child practice the items listed above so that they are prepared for their presentations on the date noted on the calendar.

Sincerely,

_____
                    Teacher

Monday	Tuesday	Wednesday	Thursday	Friday

Joke Speech

Oral Language Assessment

Student's Name: _____

Speech Components

Yes	No	Item
		States first and last name
		States complete date
		Tells a joke
		Waits an appropriate amount of time before telling the punchline of the joke

Oral Language Presentation Components

Yes	Needs Improvement	No	Item
			Speaks clearly
			Has good voice projection
			Has good eye contact
			Has good posture
			Shows evidence of having practiced the speech at home

Comments: _____

_____

Book Talk Speech

Introduction

This speech is an excellent introduction to book reports. A time line is easy to lay out for your students (see Tips for Student Success), and the required components are not too cumbersome.

Assignment

Students begin this speech by presenting basic introduction information, including their complete names and the date. Students will also present a book talk based on a book they read. Components of the book talk include the title, author's name, and a summary of the book. Students will also complete the worksheet titled Book Summary to assist them in summarizing the book and to use as a visual aid during their speeches.

Speech Components

❖ Student's complete name (first name and last name, middle name if desired)

❖ Today's date (the date of the speech)

❖ A book talk (with page 64 as a guide) telling about the book

❖ A reason that the student liked or did not like the book

☞ **Tips for Student Success** _____

Well in advance of assigning this speech, begin modeling how to complete the Book Summary worksheet. Several times a week after you read aloud a book to students, guide them through completing a summary using the frame of the worksheet. Distribute a copy of page 64 to each child. Complete the written part together, and then have the students draw pictures to correspond with each box.

Students this age are not yet capable of planning the steps and time line of what they need to do in order to complete the end task. Break the assignment into components. For example, several weeks in advance of assigning the speech, explain to students the upcoming speech assignment. When your class goes to the library that week, tell students to select a book that they will want to read and use for the speech assignment. The following week, assign reading and completing the Book Summary worksheet for homework. A week or two prior to the first child's speech presentation date, assign students to practice the components of his or her speech, using page 64 as a guide.

Book Summary Worksheet

Title   Author

Who

Did What

But

Then (or So)

At last

Book Talk Speech

Parent Letter

Dear Parents,

Presenting a formal speech is an excellent opportunity for students to develop oral language skills and to become comfortable speaking in front of a group. For this speech assignment, students will be required to present the items listed below. An example of what your child's speech may sound like is also below.

1. Child's first and last name (middle name, if desired)

2. Today's complete date (day, month, date, and year of the speech)

3. A book talk telling about a book your child has read

4. A visual aid to accompany the book talk (see the attached "Book Summary Worksheet")

5. A reason that the child liked or did not like the book

Example:

"Good morning, boys and girls. My name is Marie Chen. Today is Thursday, February 10, 2005. I would like to tell you about the book *Moondance* by Frank Asch. Bear wanted to dance with the moon. But, he danced with the clouds. Then, he danced with the rain. At last, he danced with the moon's reflection in a puddle. I enjoyed this book because the author used his imagination. I would tell my friends to read it. Thank you."

Attached is a sample of the evaluation sheet that will be used in assessing your child's speech. Please help your child practice the items listed above so that he or she is prepared for his or her presentation on the date noted on the calendar.

Sincerely,

_____

Teacher

Monday	Tuesday	Wednesday	Thursday	Friday

Book Talk Speech

Oral Language Assessment

Student's Name: _____

Speech Components

Yes	No	Item
		States first and last name
		States complete date
		States title and author of book
		Plot summary includes beginning, middle, and end
		Visual aid is neat and complete

Oral Language Presentation Components

Yes	Needs Improvement	No	Item
			Speaks clearly
			Has good voice projection
			Has good eye contact
			Has good posture
			Shows evidence of having practiced the speech at home

Comments: _____

_____

_____

Patriotic Speech

Introduction

Assigning a Patriotic Speech is an excellent way to introduce students to famous quotations important to the United States or songs that relate to our country. Although this speech may be assigned during any month, February (which has Presidents' Day) or May (which has Memorial Day) are months you may want to consider for a Patriotic Speech assignment.

Assignment

Students begin this speech by presenting basic introduction information, including their complete name and the date. Students are also required to recite the Pledge of Allegiance. In addition, students will select a patriotic quotation to recite or sing a patriotic song.

Speech Components

- ✤ Student's complete name (first name and last name, middle name if desired)

- ✤ Today's date (the date of the speech)

- ✤ Recites the Pledge of Allegiance

- ✤ Recites a patriotic saying or sings a patriotic song

☞ Tips for Student Success

Consider beginning early in the school year to prepare students for this speech assignment. Saying the Pledge of Allegiance and singing a patriotic song in school each day is a law in many states. Help expose students to a variety of patriotic quotations and songs by selecting a different one each month on which to focus. Chart the words to the quotations and songs included as suggestions for this speech assignment. Use the chart to help students learn the words as you say the quotation or sing the song each day after reciting the Pledge of Allegiance. If a different quotation or song is learned each month, by the time this speech assignment is given, students will have no problem committing one to memory.

Patriotic Quotations and Songs

The Pledge of Allegiance

I pledge allegiance to the Flag
of the United States of America,
and to the Republic for which it stands:
one Nation under God, indivisible,
With Liberty and Justice for all.

Patriotic Sayings

We hold these truths to be self-evident: that all men are created equal, that they are endowed by their Creator with certain inalienable rights, that among these are life, liberty, and the pursuit of happiness.
~ Thomas Jefferson

Four score and seven years ago, our fathers brought forth on this continent a new nation, conceived in liberty, and dedicated to the proposition that all men are created equal.
~ Abraham Lincoln

I have a dream that one day this nation will rise up and live out the true meaning of its creed: "We hold these truths to be self-evident: that all men are created equal."
~ Martin Luther King, Jr.

Patriotic Songs

You're a Grand Old Flag

You're a grand old flag, you're a high flying flag;
And forever in peace may you wave;
You're the emblem of the land I love,
The home of the free and the brave.
Every heart beats true for the Red, White, and Blue,
Where there's never a boast or brag;
But, should old acquaintance be forgot.
Keep your eye on the grand old flag.

There Are Many Flags

There are many flags in many lands,
There are flags of every hue.
But there is no flag however grand,
Like our old Red, White, and Blue.
Then hurrah for the flag, our country's flag,
Its stripes and white stars, too.
There is no flag in any land like our own
Red, White, and Blue.

Three Cheers for the Red, White, and Blue

Three cheers for the Red, White, and Blue,
Three cheers for the Red, White, and Blue!
The flag of America forever,
Three cheers for the Red, White, and Blue!

Patriotic Speech

Parent Letter

Dear Parents,

Presenting a formal speech is an excellent opportunity for students to develop oral language skills and to become comfortable speaking in front of a group. On this speech assignment, students will be required to present the items listed below. An example of what your child's speech may sound like is also below.

1. Child's first and last name (middle name, if desired)

2. Today's complete date (day, month, date, and year of the speech)

3. Recites the Pledge of Allegiance

4. Recites a patriotic saying or sings a patriotic song (see the attached "Patriotic Quotations and Songs" sheet for ideas)

Example:

"Good morning, boys and girls. My name is Kim Williams. Today is Wednesday, March 9, 2005. I would like to recite the Pledge of Allegiance for you. I pledge allegiance to the Flag of the United States of America, and to the Republic for which it stands: one Nation under God, indivisible, with Liberty and Justice for all. I will now recite for you a quote by Martin Luther King: 'I have a dream that one day this nation will rise up and live out the true meaning of its creed: "We hold these truths to be self-evident: that all men are created equal." Thank you.'"

Attached is a sample of the evaluation sheet that will be used in assessing your child's speech. Please help your child practice the items listed above so that he or she is prepared for his or her presentation on the date noted on the calendar.

Sincerely,

_____
Teacher

Monday	Tuesday	Wednesday	Thursday	Friday

Patriotic Speech

Oral Language Assessment

Student's Name: _____

Speech Components

Yes	No	Item
		States first and last name
		States complete date
		Recites the Pledge of Allegiance
		Recites a patriotic saying or sings a patriotic song

Oral Language Presentation Components

Yes	Needs Improvement	No	Item
			Recites the Pledge of Allegiance with expression and appropriate phrasing
			Recites patriotic quotation or sings patriotic song with expression and appropriate phrasing
			Speaks clearly
			Has good voice projection
			Has good eye contact
			Has good posture
			Shows evidence of having practiced the speech at home

Comments: _____

Demonstration Speech

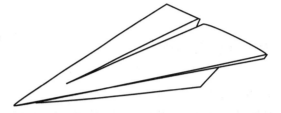

Introduction

By giving a demonstration speech, students are able to show something they know how to do or something that they know how to work. This assignment gets students thinking about how to break down a task into smaller steps.

Assignment

Students begin this speech by presenting basic introduction information, including their complete names and the date. Students will also provide a demonstration of how to do something or how something works. A visual aid or demonstration done as part of the speech is also required. If it is appropriate to their speeches, encourage students to bring props to aid in their demonstrations. For example, if a student is going to demonstrate how to brush his or her teeth, he or she can bring a toothbrush, toothpaste, and a cup to use during his or her speech.

Speech Components

* ❖ Student's complete name (first name and last name, middle name if desired)

* ❖ Today's date (the date of the speech)

* ❖ Demonstration of how to do something or how something works

☞ Tips for Student Success

Demonstrate how to break down a task into smaller pieces by practicing with students. The tasks you demonstrate can be simple and can be part of your daily routine. For example, when lining up for recess, demonstrate how you could break that task into smaller parts.

Step 1: Stand up.

Step 2: Push in chair.

Step 3: Walk to the door.

Step 4: Stand behind another student facing the door.

Another way to help students be successful with this task is to help them select topics to demonstrate about which they have much prior knowledge. Provided on page 72 is a list of topics you may wish to have students consider.

Demonstration Speech

Topic Suggestions

How to solve a math problem	How to do a card or magic trick
How to take a dog for a walk	How to make yourself breakfast
How to make a paper airplane	How to play the violin (or other instrument)
How to make a friend	How to tie your shoe
How to brush your teeth	How to make your mother (or any other person) happy

Demonstration speeches do not have to be serious. Consider some funny topics, such as those listed below.

How to annoy your little brother	How to lose your jacket
How to get put on restriction	How to trick your friend on April Fools' Day
How to get your new clothes dirty	How to get a tummy ache

Demonstration Speech

Parent Letter

Dear Parents,

Presenting a formal speech is an excellent opportunity for students to develop oral language skills, and to become comfortable speaking in front of a group. For this speech assignment, students will be required to present the items listed below. An example of what your child's speech may sound like is also below.

1. Child's first and last name (middle name, if desired)

2. Today's complete date (day, month, date, and year of the speech)

3. Demonstrate how to do something or how to work something (For example, students may want to demonstrate how to solve a math problem or how to make a peanut butter and jelly sandwich.)

Example:

"Good morning, boys and girls. My name is Maria Marquez. Today is Monday, April 18, 2005. I would like to demonstrate how to solve an addition problem for you. The problem is 24 + 31. First, write down the problem so that the ones column and the tens column are lined up. [*Student holds up a piece of paper and writes the problem on it large enough for the audience to see.*] Then, add the numbers in the ones column. [*Student demonstrates by pointing to the two numbers in the ones column.*] Write down the sum of those two numbers where the answer goes in the ones column. [*Student writes the sum in the appropriate place.*] Next, add the numbers in the tens column. [*Student demonstrates by pointing to the two numbers in the tens column.*] Write down the sum of those two numbers where the answer goes in the tens column. [*Student writes the sum in the appropriate place.*] The answer is 55. Thank you."

Attached is a sample of the evaluation sheet that will be used in assessing your child's speech. Please help your child practice the items listed above so that he or she is prepared for his or her presentation on the date noted on the calendar.

Sincerely,

_____

Teacher

Monday	Tuesday	Wednesday	Thursday	Friday

Demonstration Speech

Oral Language Assessment

Student's Name: _____

Speech Components

Yes	No	Item
		States first and last name
		States complete date
		Demonstrates how to do something or how to work something
		Provides a visual aid or demonstration to accompany speech

Oral Language Presentation Components

Yes	Needs Improvement	No	Item
			Speaks clearly
			Has good voice projection
			Has good eye contact
			Has good posture
			Shows evidence of having practiced the speech at home

Comments: _____

_____

Reciting-a-Poem Speech

Introduction

Memorizing a lengthier poem can be a challenge for some students; however, with practice, students are able to be successful in giving this speech.

Assignment

The goal with this speech is to have students memorize a poem. Provide students with a list of 4–6 poems from which they can select to memorize. You may have some favorite poems you already use in your classroom, or you can select poems out of the books recommended below.

Speech Components

❖ Student's complete name (first name and last name, middle name if desired)

❖ Today's date (the date of the speech)

❖ A memorized poem

☞ **Tips for Student Success**

Select poems related to a topic of current study. For example, if your students are learning about plants, select poems related to seeds, gardening, or plants. Songs may also be appropriate and will aid students in learning the words. If you select poems related to a topic of study, chart the words to the poems that the students have to select from and use those charts as part of shared reading lessons or read daily with the students as part of building reading fluency. Repetition and practice in the classroom will assist students in memorizing the poems they select.

Suggested Poetry Books

Below is a list of excellent poetry resources that can be used to locate poems:

Cole, Joanna. *Anna Banana: 101 Jump Rope Rhymes*. William Morrow, 1989.

de Regniers, B.S. *Sing a Song of Popcorn*. Scholastic, 1988.

Frank, Josette. *Poems to Read to the Very Young*. Random House, 2000.

Prelutsky, Jack. *The New Kid on the Block*. Greenwillow, 1984.

————. *A Pizza the Size of the Sun*. Greenwillow, 1996.

————. *The Random House Book of Poetry for Children*. Random House, 1983.

————. *Read Aloud Rhymes for the Very Young*. Knopf, 1986.

Stevenson, Robert Louis. *A Child's Garden of Verses*. Franklin Watts, 1966.

Silverstein, Shel. *A Light in the Attic*. HarperCollins Publishers, 1981.

————. *Where the Sidewalk Ends*. HarperCollins Publishers, 1974.

Reciting-a-Poem Speech

Parent Letter

Dear Parents,

Presenting a formal speech is an excellent opportunity for students to develop oral language skills and to become comfortable speaking in front of a group. On this speech assignment, students will be required to present the items listed below. An example of what your child's speech may sound like is also below.

1. Child's first and last name (middle name, if desired)

2. Today's complete date (day, month, date, and year of the speech)

3. A memorized poem

Example:

"Good morning, boys and girls. My name is Jose Marquez. Today is Monday, May 2, 2005. I would like to recite the poem 'Growing a Plant' for you today. 'Dig a little hole. Plant a little seed. Add some sun and water and wait very patiently. Underneath the ground, the roots will start to grow. After a little while, a stem will start to show. The stem will grow up taller. And leaves begin to form. A bud turns into a flower. That's how a plant is born.' Thank you."

Attached are the words to poems your child can choose from. Please read each of the poems with your child and help him/her select one from which to choose. Also attached is a sample of the evaluation sheet that will be used in assessing your child's speech. Please help your child practice the items listed above so that he or she is prepared for his or her presentation on the date noted on the calendar.

Sincerely,

_____

Teacher

Monday	Tuesday	Wednesday	Thursday	Friday

Reciting a Poem Speech

Oral Language Assessment

Student's Name: _____

Speech Components

Yes	No	Item
		States first and last name
		States complete date
		Recites a memorized poem

Oral Language Presentation Components

Yes	Needs Improvement	No	Item
			Speaks with expression
			Speaks at an appropriate speed
			Speaks clearly
			Has good voice projection
			Has good eye contact
			Has good posture
			Shows evidence of having practiced the speech at home

Comments: _____

_____

_____

Favorite Memory Speech

Introduction

A Favorite Memory Speech is an excellent speech to assign at the end of the school year. It provides students an opportunity to reflect on all of the activities that have gone on in the classroom during the previous year. It is also interesting to see what students remember and appreciated the most. Their favorite memories may surprise you!

Assignment

Students begin this speech by presenting basic introduction information including their complete names and the date. Next, students state favorite memories, along with several details about the memories. Finally, students tell why the events or memories were their favorites.

Speech Components

❖ Student's complete name (first name and last name; middle name, if desired)

❖ Today's date (the date of the speech)

❖ Student states a favorite event or memory from the school year

❖ Student tells several details from the favorite event or memory

❖ Student provides a reason why he or she chose the event or memory as a favorite

☞ Tips for Student Success

The key to students success with this speech is helping them remember events and activities from earlier in the school year. Brainstorm and chart events students remember from earlier in the school year. You may need to help jog their memories, especially of events that happened very early on in the school year. Although major events that surrounded holidays, assemblies, and field trips are bound to come up, encourage students to think about other things they enjoyed, as well. For example, students may suggest that they liked doing science experiments or getting together with book buddies on a monthly basis.

If you plan to use this speech in upcoming years, a fun way to document classroom events is to create a time line of major events as they happen. Take pictures and/or write brief sentences on index cards about major classroom or school events and post them in a time line that wraps the classroom. The time line becomes an excellent resource for ideas when this speech is assigned.

Favorite Memory Speech

Parent Letter

Dear Parents,

Presenting a formal speech is an excellent opportunity for students to develop oral language skills and to become comfortable speaking in front of a group. For this speech assignment, students will be required to present the items listed below. An example of what your child's speech may sound like is also below.

1. Child's first and last name (middle name, if desired)

2. Today's complete date (day, month, date, and year of the speech)

3. A favorite event/memory from the school year

4. At least two details from the event/memory

5. A reason the event/memory is a favorite

Example:

"Good morning, boys and girls. My name is Jovan Parekh. Today is Tuesday, June 14, 2005. My favorite memory from first grade was our field trip to the farm. We went to Centennial Farm in February. I enjoyed seeing all of the farm animals and learning about how a farm works. My favorite animals were the pigs. I liked them because the mother pigs had babies. The babies are called piglets. I would like to visit the farm again with my family. Thank you."

Attached is a sample of the evaluation sheet that will be used in assessing your child's speech. Please help your child practice the items listed above so that he or she is prepared for his or her presentation on the date noted on the calendar.

Sincerely,

_____
                    Teacher

Monday	Tuesday	Wednesday	Thursday	Friday

Favorite Memory Speech
Oral Language Assessment

Student's Name: _____

Speech Components

Yes	No	Item
		States first and last name
		States complete date
		States a favorite memory from the school year
		States at least two details from favorite memory
		States a reason the memory is a favorite

Oral Language Presentation Components

Yes	Needs Improvement	No	Item
			Speaks with expression
			Speaks at an appropriate speed
			Speaks clearly
			Has good voice projection
			Has good eye contact
			Has good posture
			Shows evidence of having practiced the speech at home

Comments: _____